Grades 6–8 Viola

Improve your sight-reading!

Paul Harris

Grade 6

Stage 1 **Introducing F minor, flat keys,** 𝄽 *page 4*

Stage 2 **More sharp keys, triplets** *page 8*

Stage 3 **9/8 and more 6/8 patterns** *page 12*

Stage 4 **5/4 and 5/8, exploring 𝄞** *page 16*

Grade 7

Stage 1 **Introducing C♯ minor** *page 20*

Stage 2 **Introducing B minor, extending the range to B** *page 24*

Stage 3 **7/8 and 7/4, left-hand pizzicato** *page 28*

Stage 4 **Revision** *page 32*

Grade 8

Stage 1 **Introducing B major, extending the range to C** *page 34*

Stage 2 **Flat keys, introducing D♭ major, ornaments** *page 38*

Stage 3 **More compound and irregular time signatures, 12/8, cross rhythms** *page 42*

Stage 4 **Revision** *page 46*

ff FABER MUSIC

Here is some guidance as to what should be in your mind as you prepare to give a musical performance when sight-reading:

- **Choose a suitable tempo** A lighter approach can help in giving the impression of speed whereas a more sustained quality of sound is appropriate in slower music.

- **Keep the pulse even and steady** If you follow the instructions in this book to count two bars in you'll have no trouble establishing a steady pulse. This will also help any musical *rubato* (appropriate in many styles of music) to sound more convincing.

- **Give energy to the rhythm** Use occasional (and usually unmarked) accentuation to help drive the music forward.

- **Shape the phrases** Gentle (unmarked) *crescendos* when ascending and *diminuendos* when descending often help to shape phrases. Try to think where each phrase is leading to.

- **Follow dynamics and other markings** These are very important in helping to bring music to life. Add more of your own if you feel they would enhance the character or add more personality to the performance. Having spoken to a number of viola teachers we've opted not to include fingering.

- **Think in the key** In your sight-reading practice, always play the scale and arpeggio (preferably from notation) as part of your preparation.

- **Give musical character to your performance** Just like an actor gets 'in character' before a performance, think about what you want to convey and keep this strongly in mind as you play. Develop your ability to understand what a piece is saying before you begin playing.

For online audio of all the Going Solo pieces scan the QR code or go to fabermusic.com/audio

With many thanks to Gillian Secret and Jessica O'Leary for their invaluable help.

© 2024 by Faber Music Ltd
This edition first published in 2024 by Faber Music Ltd.
Brownlow Yard, 12 Roger Street, London WC1N 2JU
Music processed by Donald Thomson
Cover and page design by Liz Ogden and Susan Clarke
Printed in England by Caligraving Ltd
All rights reserved

ISBN10: 0-571-54327-8
EAN13: 978-0-571-54327-4

To buy Faber Music publications or to find out about the full range of titles available please contact your local music retailer or Faber Music sales enquiries:

Faber Music Ltd, Burnt Mill, Elizabeth Way, Harlow CM20 2HX
Tel: +44 (0) 1279 82 89 82
fabermusic.com

Introduction

Being a good sight-reader is so important and it's not difficult at all! If you work through this book carefully – always making sure that you really understand each exercise before you play it – you'll never have problems learning new pieces or doing well at sight-reading in exams!

Using the workbook

1 Rhythmic exercises
Make sure you have grasped these fully before you go on to the melodic exercises: it is vital that you really know how the rhythms work. There are a number of ways to do the exercises – see *Improve your sight-reading* Grade/Level 1 for more details.

2 Melodic exercises
These exercises use just the notes (and rhythms) for the Stage, and are organised into Sets which progress gradually. If you want to sight-read fluently and accurately, get into the simple habit of working through each exercise in the following ways before you begin to play it:
- Make sure you understand the rhythm and counting. Clap the exercise through.
- Know what notes you are going to play and the fingering you are going to use.
- Try to hear the piece through in your head. Always play the first note to help.

3 Prepared pieces
Work your way through the questions first, as these will help you to think about or 'prepare' the piece. Don't begin playing until you are pretty sure you know exactly how the piece goes.

4 Going solo!
It is now up to you to discover the clues in this series of practice pieces. Give yourself about a minute and do your best to understand the piece before you play. Check the rhythms and hand position, and try to hear the piece in your head. Always remember to feel the pulse and to keep going steadily once you've begun.

The **online audio** is for you to listen to *after* you have performed any Going Solo piece. Use it to check whether you have understood the rhythm and overall feel and style of the piece correctly.

Good luck and happy sight-reading!

Terminology:
Bar = measure

Grade 6 Stage 1

Introducing F minor
Flat keys

Rhythmic exercises

Develop your inner metronome by hearing rhythmical subdivisions.
Hear each exercise in your head before clapping.

Melodic exercises

Set 1: Exploring F minor

Grade 6 Stage 1

Andante

Allegro alla Baroque

Set 2: Exploring other flat keys and 𝄾

Tastily

Gently

Prepared pieces

1 Play the scale and arpeggio in a variety of dynamics from the piece and then in the style of the piece.
2 Choose a suitable rhythmic pattern (of about two bars) and hear it in your head. Now improvise a short piece on the rhythm.
3 Think through how you will finger the piece. Then think through the bowing.
4 Tap the pulse and think the rhythm, then tap the rhythm and think the pulse.
5 Give a performance in your head, then play the piece with great confidence.

Spaghetti tarantella

Stand up

Grade 6 Stage 1

Going solo! Don't forget to prepare each piece carefully before you play it.

Look before you leap

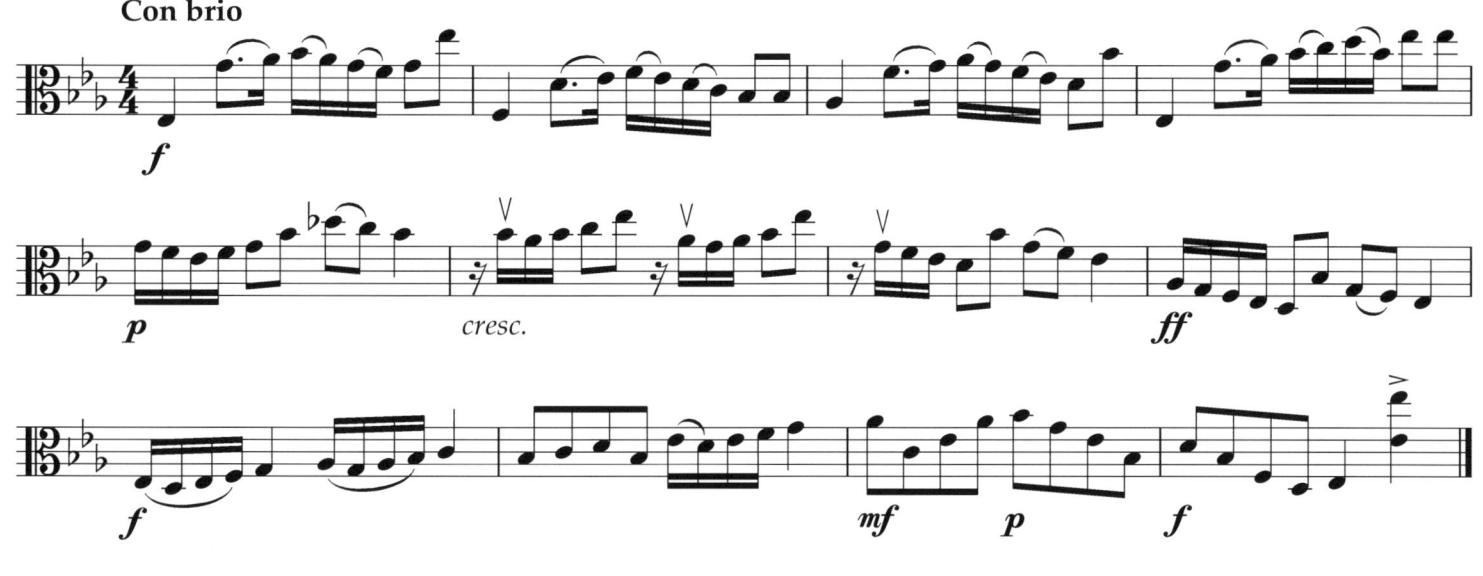

In a hurry

With a hint of JSB

Grade 6 Stage 2

More sharp keys
Triplets

Rhythmic exercises

Try assigning different sounds to each line: e.g. pizz. double bass for the lower line and side drum for the upper.

Melodic exercises

Set 1: Exploring triplets in major keys

Grade 6 Stage 2

Set 2: Exploring triplets in minor keys

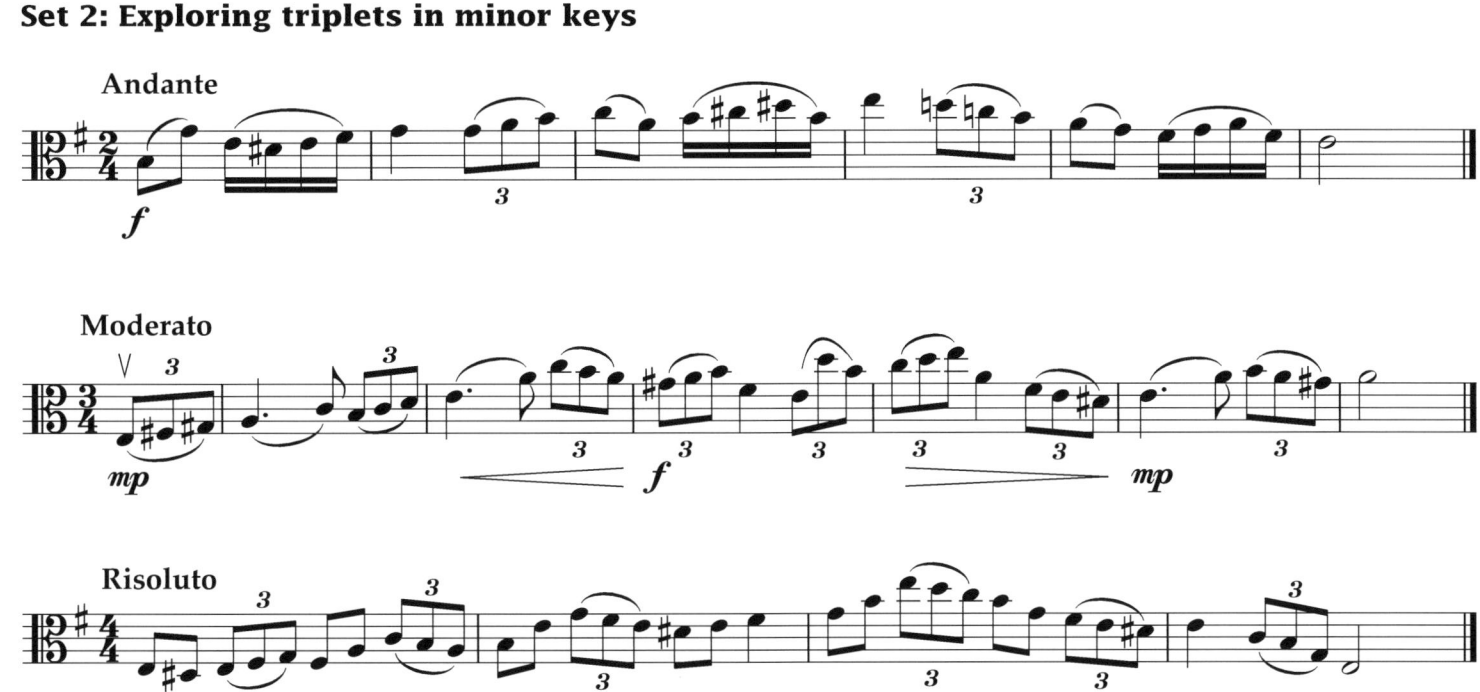

Set 3: Exploring more sharp keys

Prepared pieces

1 Play the scale and arpeggio in the character of the piece.
2 Walk around the room in time, and think or sing the rhythm.
3 Think through the bowing of the piece, in particular the bow speed.
4 Make up an exercise or short piece which continually alternates ♪♪ and ♪♪♪.
5 Play the first note and hear the piece through in your head, with musical expression.

Enjoy your triplet!

Three for the price of two

Grade 6 Stage 2

Going solo! Don't forget to prepare each piece carefully before you play it.

Waiting for a bus

Don't triplet over

Grade 6 Stage 3

9/8 and more
6/8 patterns

Rhythmic exercises

Melodic exercises

Set 1: Exploring 9/8 time

Remember to feel the ♩. pulse or ♪ subdivision.

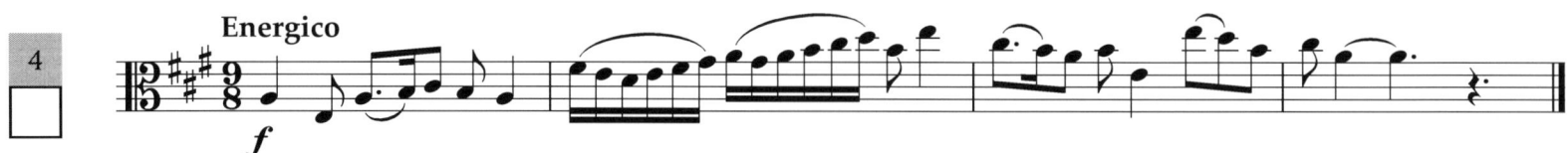

Grade 6 Stage 3

Set 2: Exploring more rhythms in 6/8 and 9/8

Prepared pieces

1 Play the scale and arpeggio in a lively manner, using dynamics from the piece.
2 How many repeated patterns can you find?
3 What will you count? Tap the pulse strongly and think the rhythm, then tap the rhythm softly and think the pulse loudly.
4 Improvise in the key in $\frac{9}{8}$ time. Make your improvisation quite long so you can immerse yourself in the music.
5 Play the first note and hear the piece through in your head, including musical expression.

Busy texting

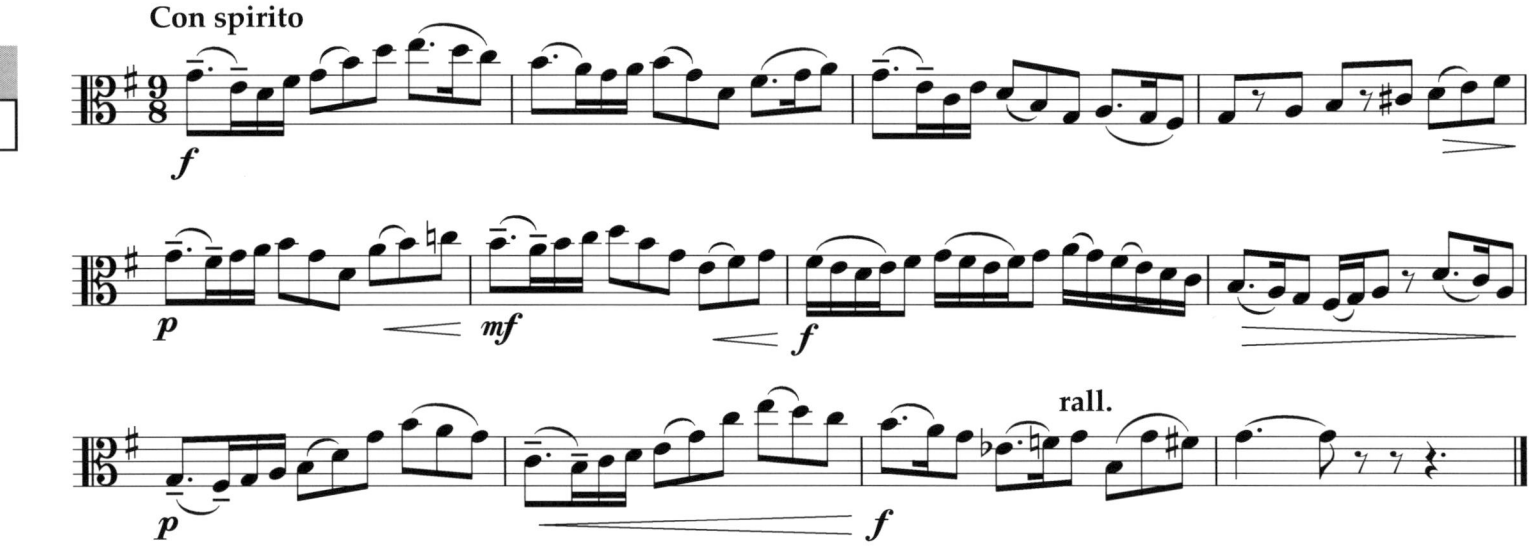

Magic spell

Grade 6 Stage 3

Going solo! Try this activity to prepare these pieces. Scan through the piece quickly (10–20 seconds), trying to absorb as much detail as you can. Then improvise a short piece using those ingredients. For more on this see 'Activity X: An exercise in creative fusion' in *How to Sight-read*.

Ballet of the Bohemian bow-makers

Ballet of the scrolls and chin-rests

Grade 6 Stage 4

Exploring 5/4 and 5/8

Rhythmic exercises

Irregular time signatures are no more difficult than regular ones. Simply keep a strong feel for the beat: ♩ in 5/4 and ♪ in 5/8. Bars will be divided into 3+2 or 2+3 groupings, which usually become apparent from the pattern of notes.

Melodic exercises

Set 1 : Exploring 5/4

Look through each piece and decide whether it is in 3+2 or 2+3 groupings.

Grade 6 Stage 4

Set 2: Exploring 5/8

Set 3: Exploring the treble clef

Prepared pieces

1 Play the scale in groups of 5.
2 Is the piece in groups of 3+2 or 2+3? How will this affect your performance?
3 Think about bowing and the fingering.
4 Tap the pulse with one hand and the rhythm with the other.
5 Play the first note and think through the performance, complete with character and dynamics.

Song and dance

Trying to ride a bicycle up a hill on a wet Wednesday evening

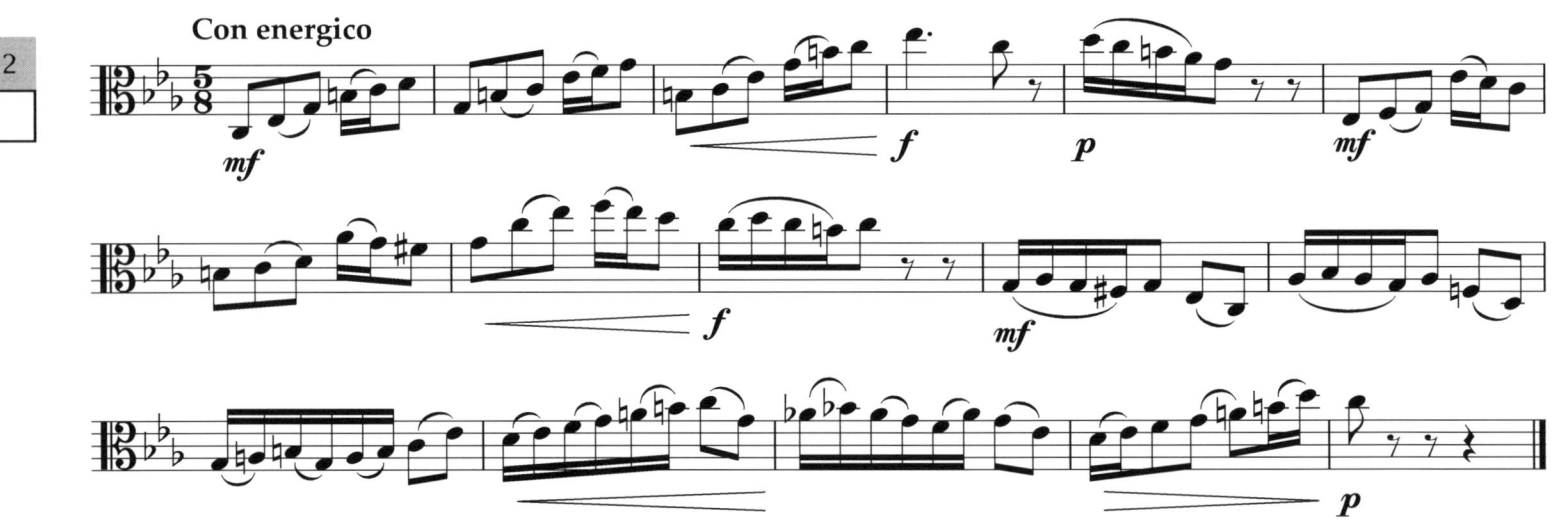

Grade 6 Stage 4

Going solo! Don't forget to prepare each piece carefully before you play it.

Don't interrupt me whilst I'm interrupting you!

Rustic loaf with marmalade

A day at the seaside

Grade 7 Stage 1

Introducing C♯ minor

Rhythmic exercises

Feel the beat and subdivisions strongly in these exercises, especially where there are ties.

1

2

3

Melodic exercises

Set 1: Exploring C♯ minor

1

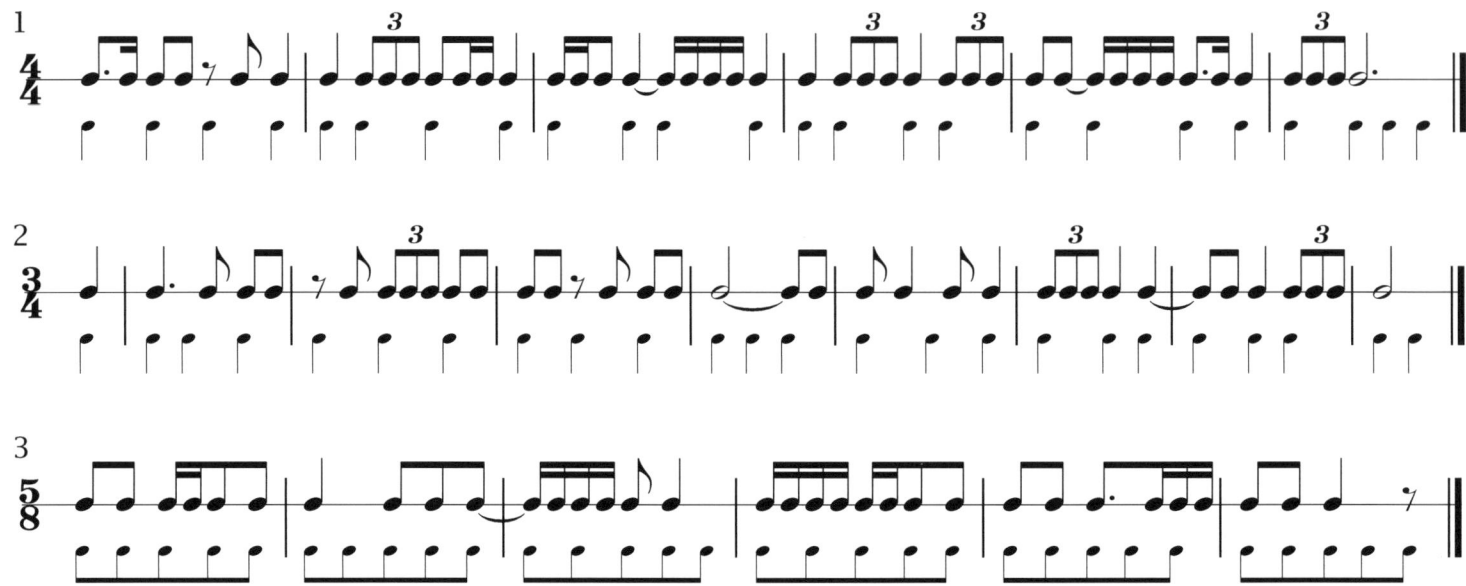

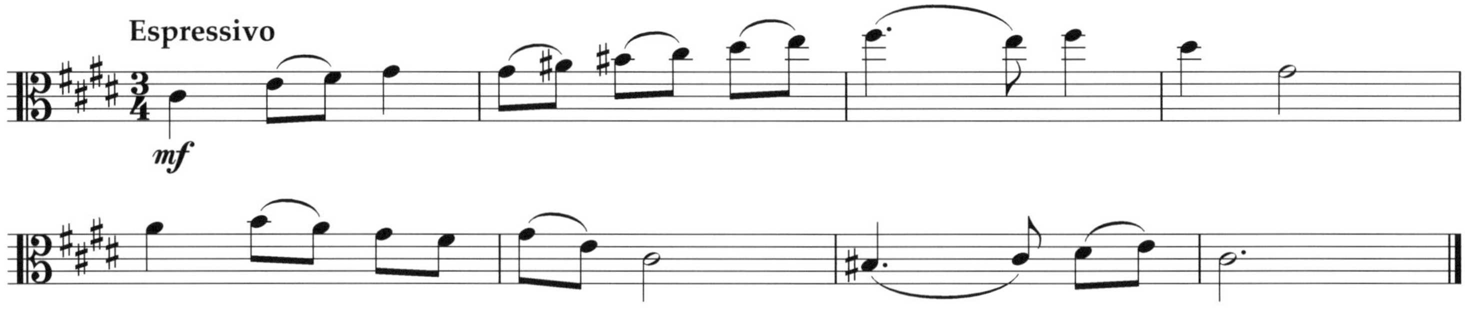

2

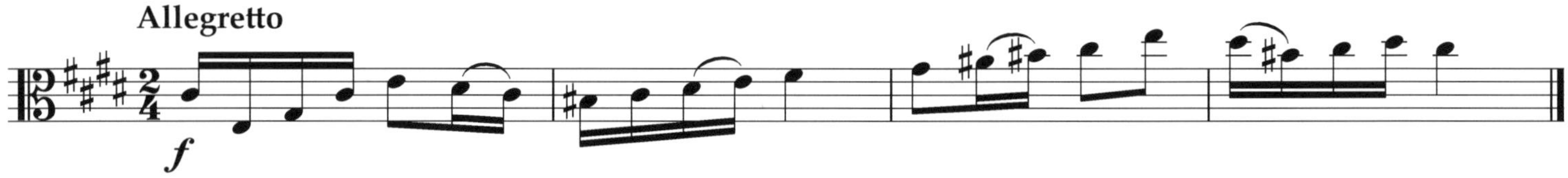

3

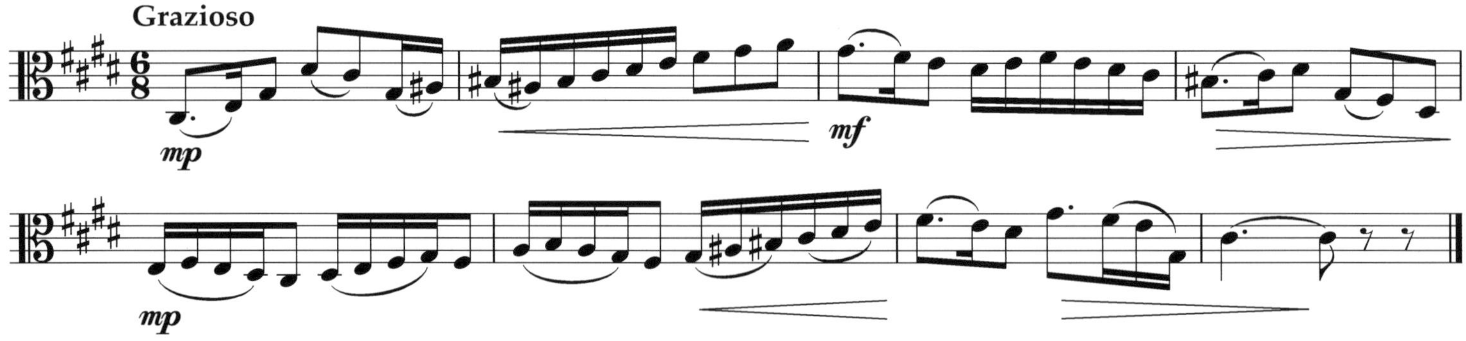

Grade 7 Stage 1

Set 2: Exploring more ties. Make sure you feel the rhythmic subdivision.

Prepared piece

1. Play the scale and arpeggio in a variety of dynamics found in this piece.
2. Hear the rhythmic pattern of the first two bars in your head. Now improvise a short piece on the rhythm.
3. Think through how you will finger the piece. Then think through the bowing.
4. Tap the pulse and think the rhythm, then tap the rhythm and think the pulse.
5. Make up an exercise based on bar 15.
6. Read the piece through silently (having played the first note), thinking about expressing the character as you do so.

Hot air ballooning on a calm day (with sandwiches)

Grade 7 Stage 1

Going solo! Don't forget to prepare each piece carefully before you play it.

Look before you leap

Dancing on the banks of the Berezayka

Not such a high five!

Grade 7 Stage 2

Introducing B minor

Extending the range to B

Rhythmic exercises

Always count two bars before you begin – one out loud and one silently.
Hear both the pulse and appropriate subdivision internally.

1

2

3

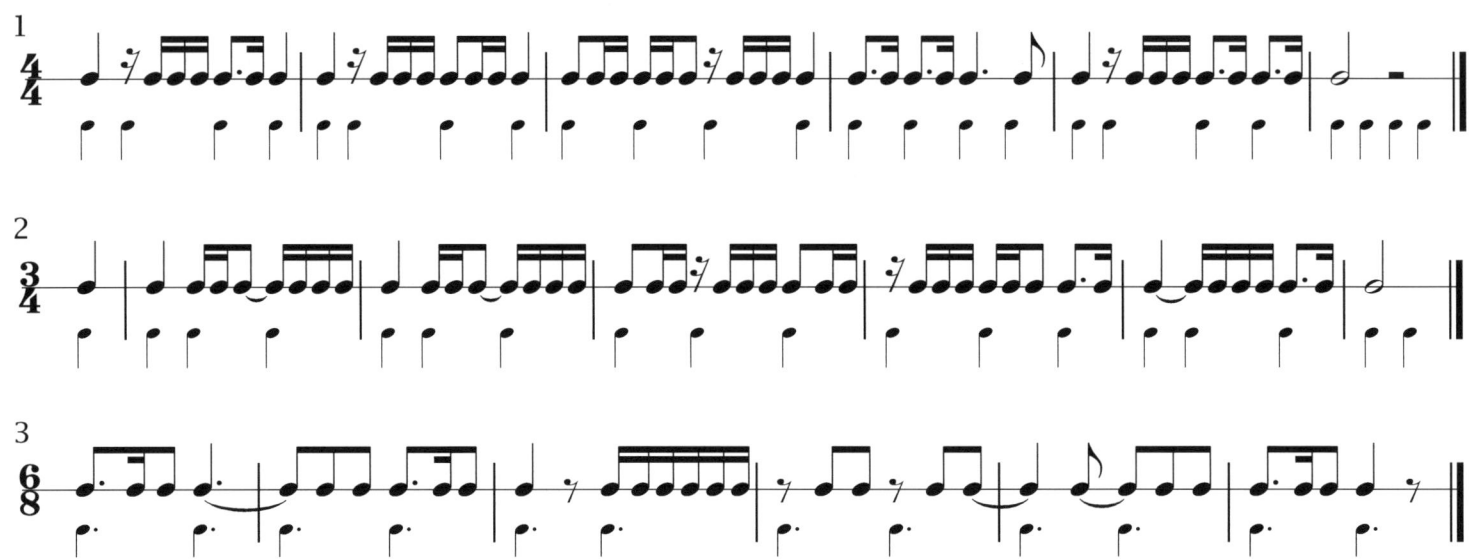

Melodic exercises

Set 1: Exploring B minor

1

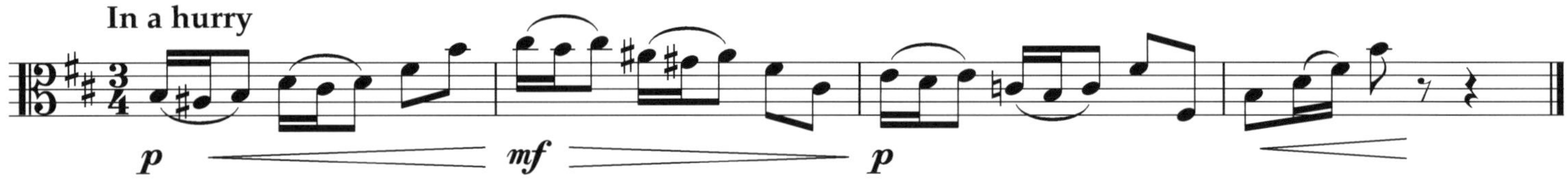
In a hurry
p
mf
p

2

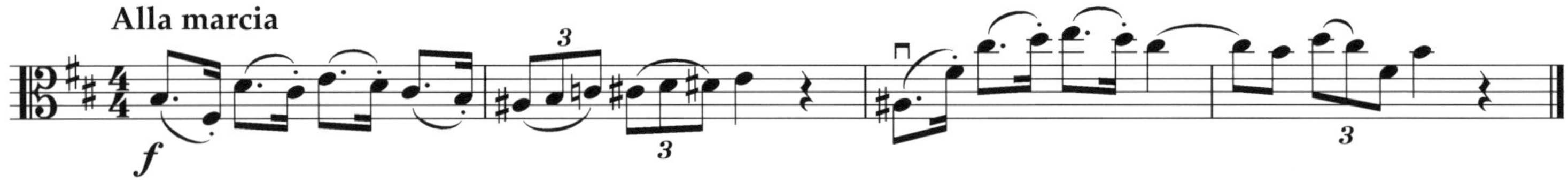
Alla marcia
f
3
3
3

3

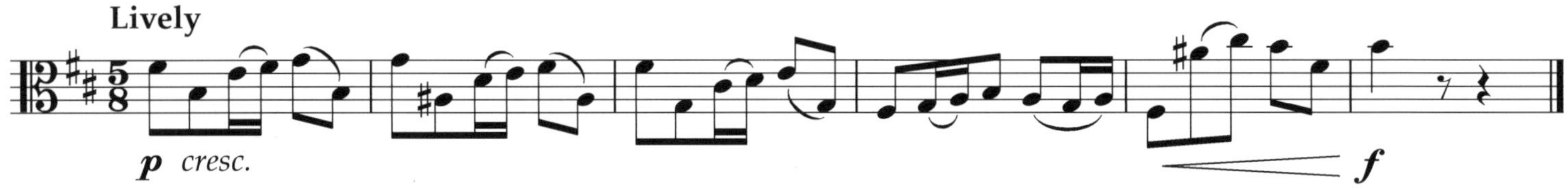
Lively
p cresc.
f

4

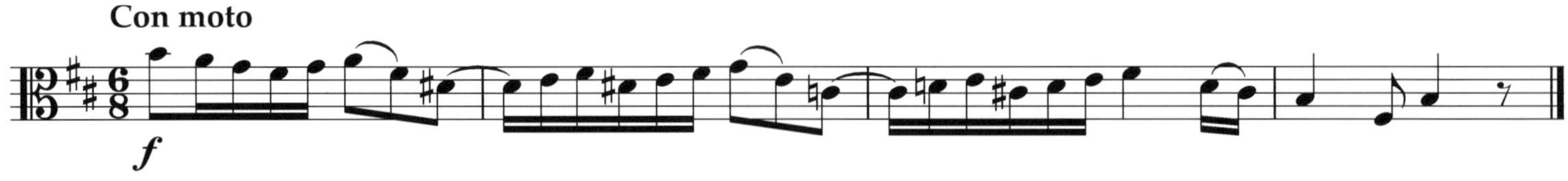
Con moto
f

Grade 7 Stage 2

Set 2: Extending the range to B

Prepared piece

> 1 Play the 3 octave scale and arpeggio in the character of the piece.
> 2 Improvise a short piece in the key, using the rhythm of the first two bars.
> 3 Think through the piece in terms of bow speed.
> 4 Think about fingering and where to shift.
> 5 Play the first note and hear the piece through in your head, with musical expression.
> 6 Now play it as if you really know the piece – with great confidence!

Four ate fish and 9/8 chicken

Grade 7 Stage 2

Going solo! Study each piece for about half a minute, then look away and see how many details you can remember.

Five go on an adventure

On a dark and stormy night ...

Grade 7 Stage 3

7/8 and 7/4
Left-hand pizzicato

Rhythmic exercises

Melodic exercises

Set 1: Exploring 7/8 time

Look out for 3+4 and 4+3 groupings in 7/8.

Prepared piece

1 Play the scale and arpeggio in the character of the piece.
2 Look at the first bar plus the next three notes for about 10 seconds, then play them from memory.
3 How many times does that pattern return?
4 Now improvise a short piece in this key, using that pattern.
5 Read the piece through in your head, in time, thinking about the fingering and shifting.
6 Feel the ♪ pulse for a couple of bars, then set off confidently and play without any hesitations.

Dance of the annoying hiccups

Grade 7 Stage 3

Going solo!
Study this piece for 30 seconds, absorbing all the details. Feel confident before you play it that the performance is going to be accurate and musical.

Dancing the night away

1

Black, no sugar

2

Grade 7 Stage 4

Revision

Brandenburg concerto no.7

1

What shall we do with the very drunk sailor?

2

From major to minor

Viola granola (with apricots)

Grade 8 Stage 1

Introducing B major
Extending the range to C

Rhythmic exercises

Remember to sense the subdivision of the pulse when needed.

Melodic exercises

Set 1: Exploring B major

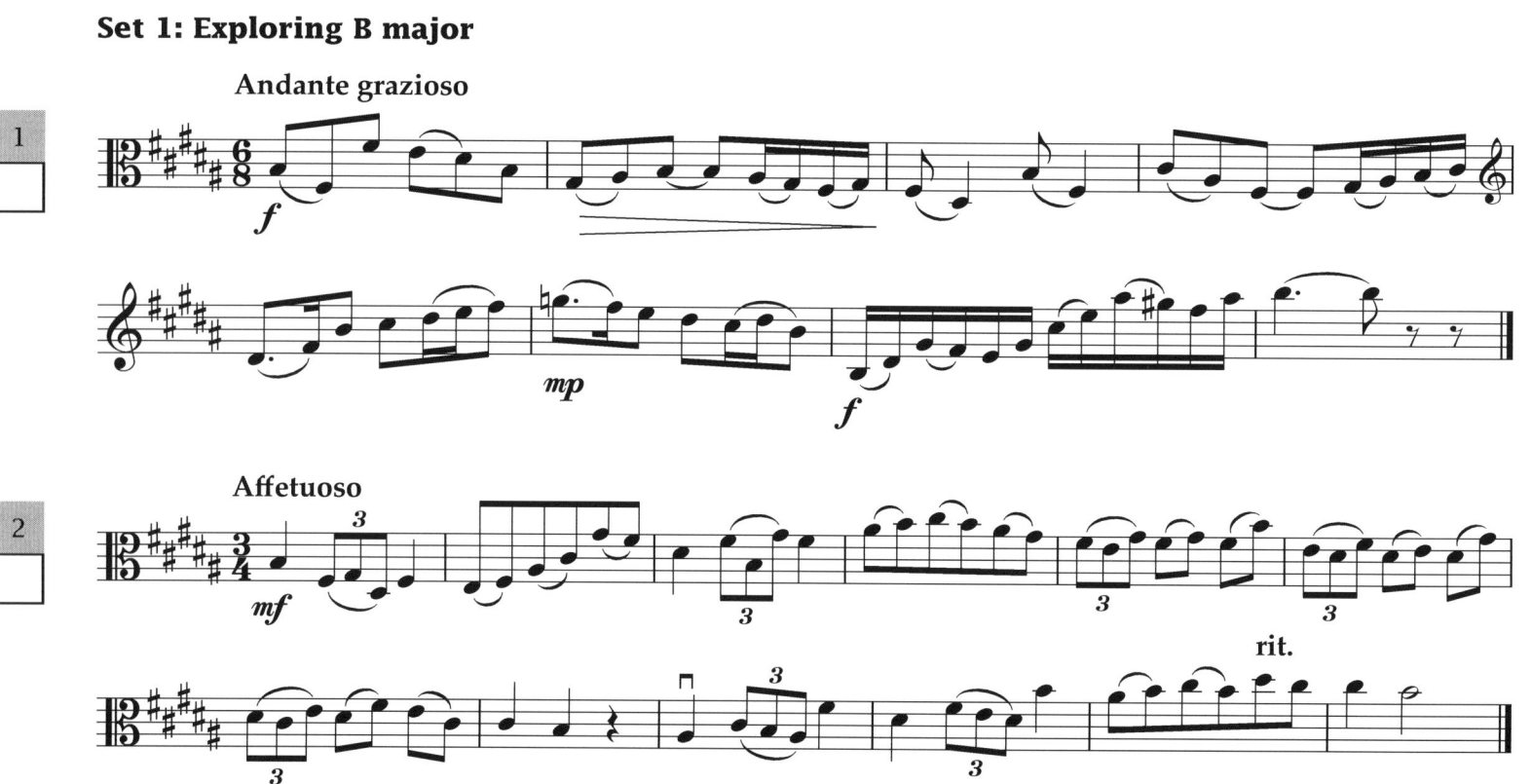

Grade 8 Stage 1

Set 2: Extending the range to top C

Prepared piece

1 Play the scale and arpeggio in an agitated character.

2 Have a look at bar 6 for about 5 seconds then play it from memory. Now improvise a piece based on that rhythm, in the same key.

3 Think through how you will finger the piece. Now think through the bowing.

4 Tap the rhythm with your left hand for bar 1, right hand for bar 2, left hand for bar 3, and so on.

5 Read through the piece confidently in your head.

6 Play the piece confidently, ignoring any slight mishaps that may occur.

Oh no, I'm late!

Grade 8 Stage 1

Going solo!
With the confidence you're developing you should be able to enjoy your performance once you begin.

Grand march from Cremona

Maggini's meditation

Grade 8 Stage 2

**Flat keys
Introducing D♭ major
Ornaments**

Rhythmic exercises

Melodic exercises

Set 1: Exploring D♭ major

Grade 8 Stage 2

Set 2: Exploring trills, grace notes and mordents

Prepared piece

1 Improvise in the key using lots of scale and arpeggio patterns and mordents.
2 Can you find where the opening music returns? How is it different?
3 Think about bow position in bars 11 and 12.
4 Tap the rhythm with one hand and a ♪ pulse with the other.
5 Play the first note and (tapping the pulse) read through the piece, hearing it in your head as accurately as you can. If you're not sure of an interval just make your best guess.
6 Study the first two bars for about 10 seconds then play the passage from memory.

Flight of fancy

Grade 8 Stage 2

Going solo! Try to breath slowly and deeply whilst preparing your performance – this will keep you calm.

Song for a lonely seafarer

1

The sky was bleak, the wind whistled, a strange wailing in the distance …

2

Grade 8 Stage 3

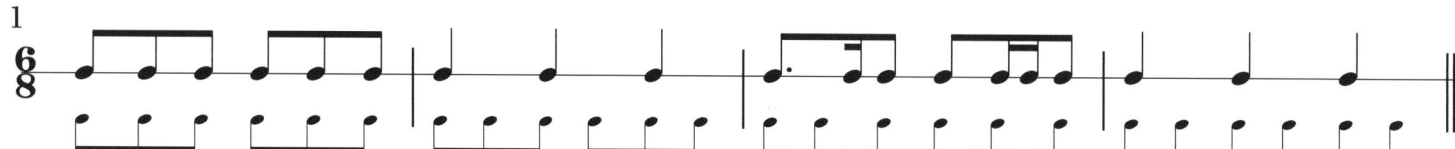

More compound and irregular time signatures
Introducing 12/8
Cross rhythms

Rhythmic exercises

1.

Compound time signatures may be felt against a ♪ or ♩. pulse, or a mixture of the two. As you become more experienced at reading these time signatures you will become adept at working out which pulse is the most appropriate.

2.

3.

Melodic exercises

Set 1: Exploring 12/8

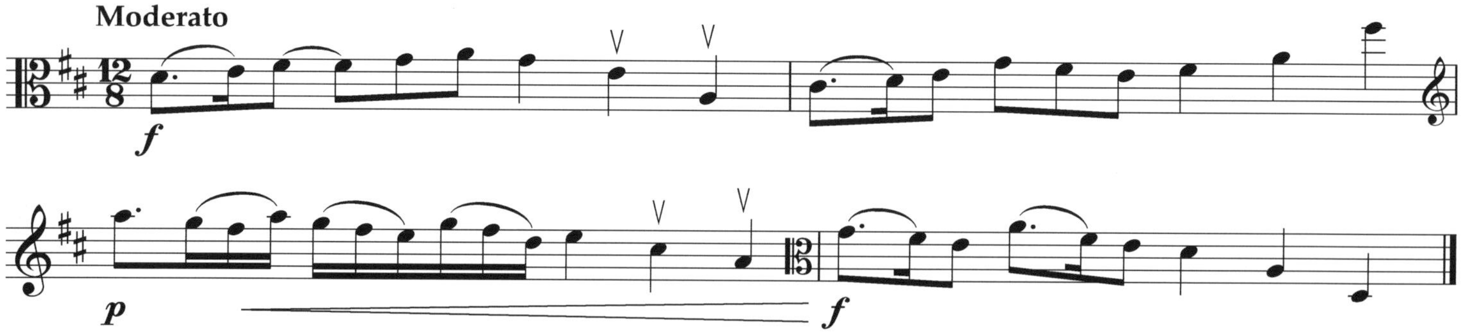

Grade 8 Stage 3

Set 2: More cross rhythms and compound time signatures

Prepared piece

1. Play all the scales and arpeggios used in this piece.
2. Scan through the piece and decide if there are any tricky rhythms. Think them through.
3. Scan again, looking for finger patterns, repeated patterns and any passages that may catch you out.
4. Read the piece through in your head, in time, hearing it as best you can.
5. Study the last bar for about 15 seconds, then play it from memory.
6. Now play the piece as if you've been learning it for months! Don't lean forward or peer at the music as you play – relax and enjoy it!

Ski-ing through the Swiss countryside

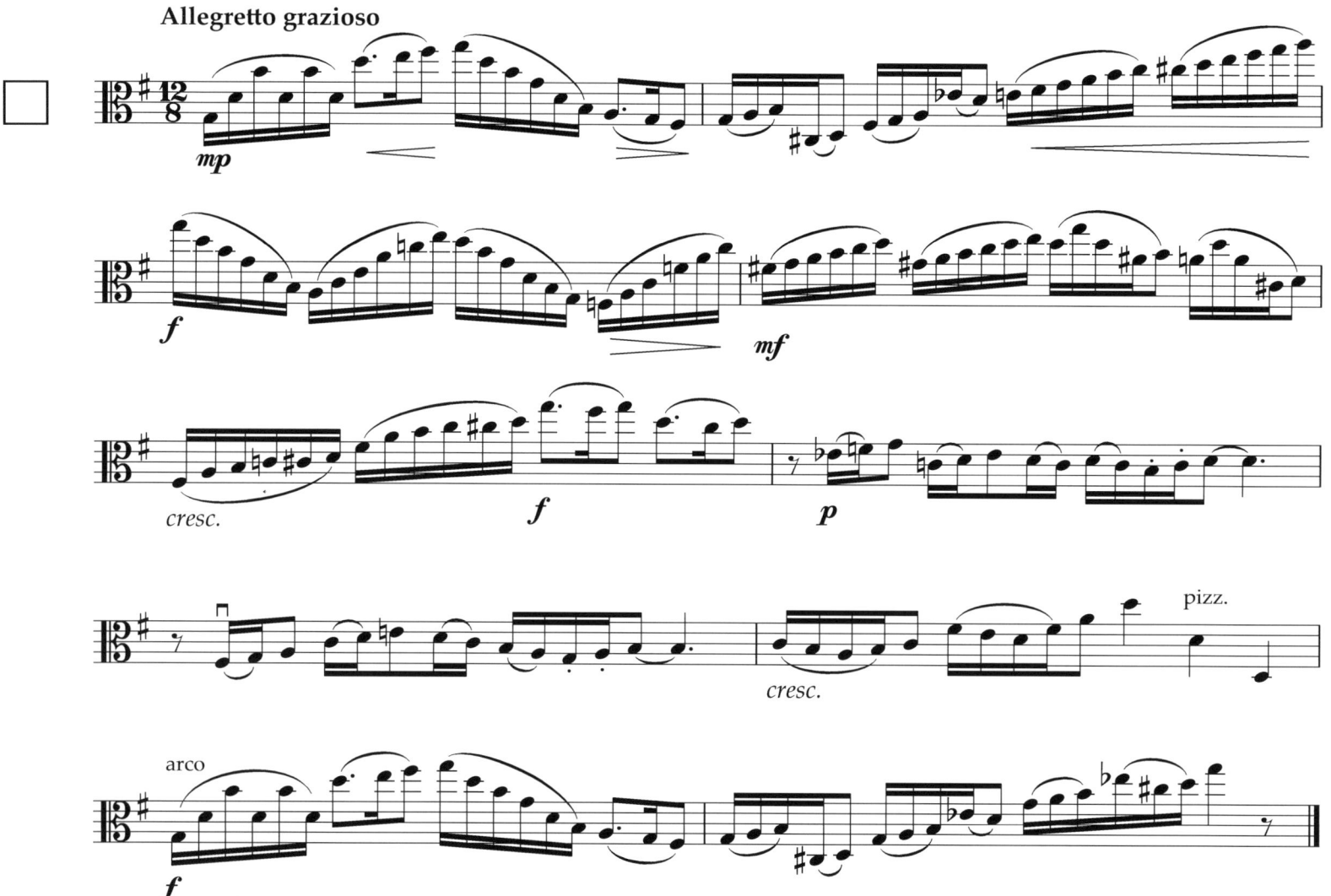

Grade 8 Stage 3

Going solo! Try playing these with a minimum of preparation – just 10 seconds and then play!

March for Martians

Here is the seven o'clock news ...

Grade 8 Stage 4

Revision

Eine kleine Tagmusik ... with a hint of Mozart

Carnival time ... with a hint of Dvořák

Pepper from The seasonings ... with a hint of Vivaldi

Transylvanian toccata ... with a hint of Bartók

Ballad ... with a hint of Malcolm Arnold

Georgie and Tess ... with a hint of Gershwin